SWEET SPOT™

Ice Cream, Frozen Desserts, and Iced Drinks

David Holcomb ❉ Lindsey Walker

ShinShinChez LLC

First edition 2014
Printed in Canada

Authors: David Holcomb, Lindsey Walker
Recipes: Dale Nelson
Editors: Marlen Boivin, Nancy Gellos
Photographer: Angie Norwood Browne
Food Stylist: Patty Wittmann
Copy Editor: Judy Gouldthorpe
Cover Design: Mint, Seattle WA
Book Design: Nancy Gellos
Publisher: ShinShinChez LLC

ISBN-13: 978-0-615-96682-3

For the kid in all of us.

Mix It Up

Sweet Memories

As a kid, I formed my earliest ice cream memories at my grandparents' house. They would lug out this wooden bucket with a motor and make a big fuss over getting the mix right with all the ice and salt. In kid time (which works a lot like dog years), the process seemed to take an eternity. And though I didn't understand how it all worked, once it was done, I swear I had never tasted anything so creamy and smooth. Come to think of it, my love for both food and gadgets may have been born here. Not long after I tasted my first batch of homemade ice cream, my grandparents caved in to my heartfelt pleas for a Veg-O-Matic, which promptly broke after one use. I knew right then that I could build something better, and I soon set out to try.

Flash forward and we are all grown, and though we still clamor for our favorite flavors, our palates may be more refined. Those of us with children want to share our ice cream dreams with the next generation, but we are also mindful of what ingredients we choose. Thankfully, the Sweet Spot allows home cooks to make a nearly infinite variety of ice creams, sherbets, and granitas while granting them full control over what goes in. We know that high-quality ingredients yield high-quality dishes, and the Sweet Spot allows discerning home chefs to create sweet masterpieces in their kitchens.

Create sweet masterpieces in the kitchen.

These recipes will no doubt be a hit at your next gathering! Easy-to-follow instructions plus lots of mix-ins mean that kids can have creative fun blending their own flavors, like Rocky Toffee Road and Peanut Butter Chocolate. And the small-batch method allows choosy eaters to mix in their own ingredients, which can vary from one scoop to the next. For adults, the Lemon Drop Ice and Margarita recipes will surely liven up their parties, too. Sure, you could always scoop store-bought ice cream from a cardboard tub, but creating your own flavors, especially with friends and family, becomes a means for also creating new, shared memories.

I hope that the recipes included here will serve as an easy guide for first-time ice cream makers just cutting their teeth on frozen treats and as an inspiration for those with more than a few sorbet batches under their belts. And though these Sweet Spot recipes are excellent on their own, don't shy away from experimenting with ingredients or servings. Why not float some Toasted Coconut in your favorite cola? Or blend a little Salted Caramel into your next iced coffee? Let your creative prowess run amok!

David Holcomb
Chef'n Founder & Famous Inventor

A love of all things swee

rings friends and family closer together.

The Sweet Spot

Pour   Add   Mix

Place your Chef'n Sweet Spot ice cream maker on a flat surface in your freezer. Allow it to freeze for a full 24 hours before making your first batch.

Pour ½ cup of your favorite ice cream recipe onto the surface. Wait approximately 2 minutes, then mix with the tools included, like you're making scrambled eggs. Keep going! Continue to fold, mix, and blend over the Sweet Spot surface until it reaches the desired texture, about 1½ to 2 minutes. This makes six ½-cup servings in less than 30 minutes.

To clean, rinse with warm water. The Sweet Spot is not dishwasher safe! Be gentle; never clean with scouring powders or hard implements. Be sure it is completely dry before placing it in the freezer.

Golden Syrup

Enjoy!

2 cups granulated sugar
2 tablespoons fresh lemon juice
1 cup warm water, divided
1 teaspoon pure vanilla extract

Pastry brush and cup of warm water

In a heavy-bottomed medium saucepan, combine the sugar, lemon juice and ½ cup warm water. Stir until the sugar starts to dissolve. Dip the pastry brush in the warm water and brush down the sides of the pan to remove any sugar crystals. This is an important step to prevent sugar crystals from forming. Bring to a rolling boil over medium-high heat and cook until the temperature is 270°F, or until it is a light golden color (about 6 to 8 minutes). Periodically brush down the sides of the pan to prevent crystals from forming. Remove from the heat. Let the bubbling die down before carefully stirring in the remaining ½ cup of water. Watch out for steam. Stir in the vanilla. Let cool to room temperature. Pour into a glass container and seal. Store at room temperature.

This simple Golden Syrup is easy to make and it stores well in your pantry for up to a year. It is used in the recipes on the following pages.

Makes about 1½ cups.

There's always a place in your heart f

14

...our first love.

BARE NECESSITIES

* Madagascar Vanilla Bean
* Strawberry
* Chocolate-Lovers' Delight
* Sweet Cream

Madagascar Vanilla Bean

Seeds from 1 vanilla bean
1½ cups whole milk
1½ cups heavy whipping cream
¾ cup granulated sugar
⅛ teaspoon sea salt
2 tablespoons golden syrup (page 13)
2 teaspoons pure vanilla extract

In a mixing bowl, combine all ingredients. Stir with
a spoon until the sugar dissolves, using a quick circular
motion without creating foam. This will take a few minutes.
Pour into a container, cover, and refrigerate until chilled.

At the time of use, stir the chilled mixture well, without creating foam,
to evenly distribute the vanilla seeds. For each serving, pour ½ cup
into the Sweet Spot. Stir until frozen and serve.

Makes six ½-cup servings.

You're the sweetest thing I ever did see.

Fresh-picked raspberries and raspberry preserves create a new version of this classic ice cream.

In the midday sun, fragrant berries shade themselves under leaves.

Strawberry

2½ cups ripe, in-season strawberries (about 25 berries),
        or unsweetened frozen strawberries, thawed
1 teaspoon plus 2 tablespoons granulated sugar
2 teaspoons fresh lemon juice, divided
1 cup whole milk
1 cup heavy whipping cream
⅔ cup strawberry preserves with bits of fruit (not low-sugar)
½ teaspoon fine sea salt
2 tablespoons golden syrup (page 13)
½ teaspoon pure vanilla extract

Wash and stem the strawberries. Chop 1 cup of the strawberries into ¼-inch pieces. Mix in a bowl with 1 teaspoon sugar and 1 teaspoon lemon juice. Refrigerate.

In a blender, puree the remaining 1½ cups berries. Transfer to a bowl and add the milk, cream, preserves, 2 tablespoons sugar, salt, golden syrup, vanilla and 1 teaspoon lemon juice. Stir with a spoon until the sugar dissolves, using a quick circular motion without creating foam. This will take a few minutes. Pour into a container, cover, and refrigerate until chilled.

For each serving, stir and then pour ½ cup of the chilled mixture into the Sweet Spot. Stir while freezing. Once it is ¾ frozen, fold in 2 tablespoons chopped strawberries.

Makes six ½-cup servings.

Chocolate-Lovers' Delight

3 ounces dark chocolate (85% cacao), cut in small pieces (or ¾ cup
      chocolate chips)
¼ cup plus ½ cup granulated sugar
¼ cup Dutch-process cocoa powder
1½ cups whole milk
1½ cups heavy whipping cream
¼ teaspoon fine sea salt
2 tablespoons golden syrup (page 13)
1 teaspoon pure vanilla extract

Place the chocolate pieces in a large heatproof mixing bowl. Set aside. In
a small bowl, blend ¼ cup sugar and the cocoa. Set aside.

In a heavy-bottomed saucepan, combine the milk, cream, ½ cup sugar, salt
and golden syrup. Stir with a spoon until the sugar begins to dissolve.
Cook over medium heat for 2 to 3 minutes, or until steam rises and small
bubbles begin to form around the edges. Remove from the heat *prior*
to boiling. Carefully pour the heated milk mixture
over the chocolate pieces. Let stand for 3 to 5
minutes to fully melt the chocolate. Whisk
until smooth. Blend in the cocoa mixture.
When fully incorporated, stir in the vanilla.
Let cool. Pour into a container, cover,
and refrigerate until chilled.

Create your own
chocolate ice cream by
choosing your favorite
type of chocolate —
it's up to you.

For each serving, stir and then pour ½ cup
of the chilled mixture into the Sweet Spot.
Stir until frozen and serve.

Makes six ½-cup servings.

Why not send a love letter to your tastebuds?

Sweet Cream

1⅓ cups whole milk
1⅔ cups heavy whipping cream
½ cup granulated sugar
¼ teaspoon fine sea salt
2 tablespoons golden syrup (page 13)
1 teaspoon pure vanilla extract

In a mixing bowl, combine the milk, cream, sugar, salt, golden syrup and vanilla. Stir with a spoon until the sugar dissolves, using a quick circular motion without creating foam. This will take a few minutes. Pour into a container, cover, and refrigerate until chilled.

For each serving, stir and then pour ½ cup of the chilled mixture into the Sweet Spot. When it is ¾ frozen, fold in your choice of mix-ins.

Makes six ½-cup servings.

Sweet Cream
is perfect for candy
mix-ins. Less sugar in the
base allows any choice
of mix-in to be enjoyed
without becoming
too sweet.

Just the basics, setting the stage for mix-in masterpieces.

A little imagination makes lasting memories.

Adventure awaits; you just have

ANY FLAVOR ANY DAY

* Mint Chocolate Chip
* Toasted Coconut
* Key Lime Pie
* Red Raspberry Cheesecake
* Peanut Butter Chocolate
* Maple Nut
* S'more
* Strawberry Maple Yogurt
* Pistachio
* Salted Caramel
* Peach Oatmeal Crisp
* Earl Grey
* Brown Butter Pecan
* Almond Fudge Ribbon
* Avocado Horchata
* Honey Lemon Sorbet
* Pineapple Spice Sorbet
* Coffee
* Coffee Toffee Malt
* Macadamia Mango Sherbet
* Rocky Toffee Road
* Chocolate Banana Malt
* Caramel Apple
* Pumpkin Pie
* Peppermint Crunch

ok for it!

Mint Chocolate Chip

1¼ cups whole milk
1¾ cups heavy whipping cream
¾ cup granulated sugar
¼ teaspoon fine sea salt
2 tablespoons golden syrup (page 13)
3 to 4 drops pure peppermint oil (see note)
3 ounces bittersweet chocolate (70% cacao), finely chopped

In a mixing bowl, combine the milk, cream, sugar, salt, golden syrup and peppermint oil. Stir with a spoon until the sugar dissolves, using a quick circular motion without creating foam. This will take a few minutes. Pour into a container, cover, and refrigerate until chilled.

For each serving, stir and then pour ½ cup of the chilled mixture into the Sweet Spot. Sprinkle with 2 tablespoons chopped chocolate. Stir until frozen and serve.

Makes six ½-cup servings.

Peppermint oil has a much more concentrated flavor than peppermint extract. You can substitute 2 teaspoons of peppermint extract for the peppermint oil in this recipe.

Out by the tire swing, the grass lights up all sun-splashed green.

Toasted Coconut

What dessert would you make

desert island?

½ cup sweetened shredded coconut
½ teaspoon plus ⅛ teaspoon fine sea salt
3 cups coconut milk
1 cup granulated sugar
2 tablespoons golden syrup (page 13)
½ teaspoon natural coconut flavor
     (or pure vanilla extract)

Preheat oven to 400°F. In a small bowl, mix the coconut and ½ teaspoon salt. Spread evenly on a lined baking sheet. Toast on the middle oven rack for 5 to 7 minutes, or until the coconut is light brown. Let cool to room temperature.

In a mixing bowl, combine the coconut milk, sugar, ⅛ teaspoon salt, golden syrup and coconut flavor. Stir with a spoon until the sugar dissolves, using a quick circular motion without creating foam. This will take a few minutes. Pour into a container, cover, and refrigerate until chilled.

Coconut milk is a non-dairy option that tastes fantastic.

For each serving, stir and then pour ½ cup of the chilled mixture into the Sweet Spot. Add a generous pinch of toasted coconut. Stir until frozen and serve.

Makes six ½-cup servings.

Key Lime Pie

2 tablespoons grated lime zest (about 4 to 6 limes)
⅓ cup lime juice (6 Key limes or 3 large limes)
2 tablespoons lemon juice (about 1 small lemon)
1 cup whole milk
1½ cups heavy whipping cream
½ cup granulated sugar
2 tablespoons golden syrup
1 teaspoon pure vanilla extract
½ cup mascarpone cheese
¾ to 1½ cups coarsely chopped graham crackers

In a large mixing bowl, combine the lime zest and juice, lemon juice, milk, cream, sugar, golden syrup and vanilla. Stir gently until the sugar dissolves. Use an open-wire whisk to slowly incorporate the cheese without creating foam. This will take a few minutes. Pour into a container, cover, and refrigerate until chilled.

For each serving, stir and then pour ½ cup of the chilled mixture into the Sweet Spot. Once it is ¾ frozen, fold in 2 to 4 tablespoons chopped graham crackers.

Makes six ½-cup servings.

For a low-fat treat, substitute softened Neufchatel cream cheese for the mascarpone, and replace the whole milk and whipping cream with low-fat milk.

Red Raspberry Cheesecake

*In morning fog, berry brambles rest
before the heat settles in.*

¼ cup (2 ounces) cream cheese, softened
¾ cup granulated sugar
1½ cups whole milk
1½ cups heavy whipping cream
¼ teaspoon fine sea salt
2 tablespoons golden syrup (page 13)
1 tablespoon grated lemon zest (1 to 2 lemons)
1 tablespoon fresh lemon juice

Garnish: Crushed graham crackers

In a bowl, mix the cream cheese and sugar until well blended. With a spoon, stir in the milk, cream, salt, golden syrup, and lemon zest and juice, using a quick circular motion without creating foam, until the sugar dissolves. This will take a few minutes. Pour into a container, cover, and refrigerate until chilled.

For each serving, stir and then pour ½ cup of the chilled mixture into the Sweet Spot. Stir until frozen. To serve, drizzle with raspberry sauce and top with crushed graham crackers.

Makes six ½-cup servings.

RED RASPBERRY SAUCE

2 cups fresh red raspberries
1 cup granulated sugar
1 tablespoon fresh lemon juice

Place all ingredients in a small, heavy-bottomed saucepan. Bring to a boil over medium-high heat, stirring, until the sugar is fully dissolved. This takes about 6 minutes. Remove from the heat and let cool. Pour into a container, cover, and refrigerate until chilled.

Peanut Butter Chocolate

1½ cups whole milk
½ cup granulated sugar
½ teaspoon fine sea salt
2 tablespoons golden syrup (page 13)
⅔ cup peanut butter, smooth or chunky
1½ cups heavy whipping cream
1 teaspoon pure vanilla extract
6 tablespoons Chocolate Fudge Topping (page 82)

In a medium saucepan, combine the milk, sugar, salt and golden syrup. Stir until the sugar dissolves. Cook over medium heat for 2 to 3 minutes, or until steam rises and small bubbles begin to form around the edges. Remove from the heat *prior* to boiling. Whisk the peanut butter into the hot milk mixture. Gently stir in the cream and vanilla. Pour into a container, cover, and refrigerate until chilled.

For each serving, stir and then pour ½ cup of the chilled mixture into the Sweet Spot. Once it is ¾ frozen, fold in 1 tablespoon Chocolate Fudge Topping.

Makes six ½-cup servings.

For a sophisticated twist, top each serving with roasted nuts. Page 80

Memories of childhood:
bag lunch, pencil shavings,
and the sound of crayons rattling in a pencil box.

Maple Nut

1½ cups whole milk
1½ cups heavy whipping cream
¾ cup dark pure maple syrup, grade B (or grade A dark amber)
2 tablespoons dark brown sugar
1 teaspoon fine sea salt
2 teaspoons pure vanilla extract

In a mixing bowl, combine all ingredients. Stir with a spoon until the sugar dissolves, using a quick circular motion without creating foam. This will take a few minutes. Pour into a container, cover, and refrigerate until chilled.

For each serving, stir and then pour ½ cup of the chilled mixture into the Sweet Spot. Stir while freezing. Once it is ¾ frozen, fold in 1 tablespoon chopped roasted walnuts.

Makes six ½-cup servings.

For a rich, smoky variation add crispy, peppered bacon bits.

OVEN-ROASTED WALNUTS

¾ cup walnut halves
1 tablespoon unsalted butter, melted
½ teaspoon fine sea salt

Preheat oven to 350°F. In a bowl, combine the nuts, butter and salt. Toss until well coated. Spread evenly on a lined sheet pan. Place the pan on the middle oven rack. Bake until lightly browned and fragrant, about 10 minutes. Let cool to room temperature, then coarsely chop. Store in a sealed container for up to 2 weeks.

In a seaside town,
there's a gingerbread house
where desserts come
on tin trays.

S'more

5 cups mini marshmallows
1½ cups whole milk, divided
1½ cups heavy whipping cream
½ cup light brown sugar
⅛ teaspoon fine sea salt
2 tablespoons golden syrup (page 13)
1 teaspoon pure vanilla extract

Mix-ins:
6 tablespoons chocolate sauce (page 83)
3 graham crackers, crumbled

Garnish:
6 tablespoons chocolate shavings

Remember the orange crackle of campfire and those starry nights off beaten trails?

Preheat the broiler. Spread the marshmallows evenly on a foil-lined sheet pan. Place under the broiler, rotating the pan for even browning. Smoke will begin to rise from the toasting. Remove from the oven as soon as the tops of the marshmallows turn a rich brown color. Be careful—they are hot and sticky. Let cool to room temperature.

In a saucepan, combine 4 cups of the toasted marshmallows with 1 cup milk. Cook over medium heat, stirring, until the marshmallows dissolve into the milk. Pour into a heatproof bowl. Add the remaining milk, cream, brown sugar, salt, golden syrup and vanilla. Stir until the sugar dissolves, using a quick circular motion without creating foam. This will take a few minutes. Pour into a container, cover, and refrigerate until chilled.

For each serving, stir and then pour ½ cup of the chilled mixture into the Sweet Spot. Stir while freezing. Once it is ¾ frozen, fold in 1 tablespoon chocolate sauce and 1 tablespoon crumbled graham crackers. To serve, garnish with the remaining toasted marshmallows and chocolate shavings.

Makes six ½-cup servings.

Strawberry Maple Yogurt

2 cups ripe, in-season strawberries (about 20 berries), or unsweetened
      frozen strawberries, thawed
⅔ cup maple syrup
1½ cups Greek yogurt, nonfat to full-fat (taster's choice)

Wash and stem the strawberries. In a blender, puree 1½ cups of the
berries. Pour the puree into a mixing bowl and whisk in the maple
syrup until it is completely blended. Add the yogurt and stir gently
until blended. Pour into a container, cover, and refrigerate until chilled.
Just prior to freezing the yogurt mixture, chop the remaining ½ cup
strawberries into ¼-inch pieces.

For each serving, stir and then pour ½ cup of the chilled mixture into
the Sweet Spot. Stir while freezing. Once it is ¾ frozen, fold in
a few of the chopped strawberries.

Makes six ½-cup servings.

Blueberries,
blackberries, or a
combination of fresh
berries make this
simple recipe fun
all season.

When it rains outside, at least we've got Sunday mornings at hom pouring over the funny pages.

43

Pistachio

½ cup roasted pistachios (page 80)
⅓ cup granulated sugar
1½ cups whole milk
⅓ cup golden syrup (page 13)
1 teaspoon fine sea salt
1½ cups heavy whipping cream
½ teaspoon natural almond extract

Garnish: Coarsely chopped roasted pistachios

Place the roasted pistachios and sugar in a food processor. Short-pulse into a fine powder, scraping down the sides of the processor so the nuts are evenly textured. Note: If the pulses are too long, the nuts will form a paste.

In a saucepan, combine the pistachio-sugar mixture and milk. Bring to a simmer over medium-high heat, stirring. Remove from the heat and let steep for 15 minutes. Stir in the remaining ingredients, using a quick circular motion without creating foam. This will take a few minutes. Pour into a container, cover, and refrigerate until chilled.

For each serving, stir and then pour ½ cup of the chilled mixture into the Sweet Spot. Stir until frozen. To serve, garnish with chopped pistachios.

Makes six ½-cup servings.

Sweet crunchiness shakes up an otherwise heavenly cream.

Salted Caramel

1 cup granulated sugar
2 tablespoons golden syrup (page 13)
¼ cup water
1 tablespoon unsalted butter
1¾ cups whole milk
1¼ cups heavy whipping cream
1½ teaspoons fine sea salt
2 teaspoons pure vanilla extract

Pastry brush and cup of warm water

The darker the caramel, the stronger the flavor.

In a heavy-bottomed medium saucepan, combine the sugar, golden syrup and water. Stir until well blended. Dip the pastry brush in the warm water and brush down the sides of the pan to remove any sugar crystals. This is an important step to prevent sugar crystals from forming. Bring to a rolling boil over medium-high heat and cook until the temperature is 305° to 315°F, about 6 to 10 minutes. It will become copper-colored and aromatic. Remove from the heat. Add the butter, stirring until incorporated. *Slowly* and carefully stir in the milk and cream. Watch out for steam. Stir in the salt and vanilla. Pour into a container, cover, and refrigerate until chilled.

For each serving, stir and then pour ½ cup of the chilled mixture into the Sweet Spot. Stir until frozen and serve.

Makes six ½-cup servings.

Shake the sand from your towel
and take a stroll up the boardwalk.

At summer's peak,
branches bend low
with plump peaches.

Peach Oatmeal Crisp

2 ripe peaches, peeled and pitted, divided
¾ cup granulated sugar
½ teaspoon ground cinnamon
1 cup whole milk
1 cup heavy whipping cream
¼ teaspoon fine sea salt
2 tablespoons golden syrup (page 13)
2 tablespoons unsalted butter

In a blender, puree 1 peach until smooth. Set aside. Take half of the 2nd peach and dice into ¼-inch pieces. Set aside.

In a large bowl, mix the sugar and cinnamon until blended. Add the milk, cream, salt and golden syrup. Stir with a spoon until the sugar dissolves, using a quick circular motion without creating foam. This will take a few minutes. Stir in the peach puree and diced peaches. Pour into a container, cover, and refrigerate until chilled.

Slice the remaining half peach. Sauté in the butter until browned. Set aside and let cool.

For each serving, stir and then pour ½ cup of the chilled mixture into the Sweet Spot. Once it is ¾ frozen, fold in 1 tablespoon Oatmeal Crisp. Garnish with a sautéed peach slice.

Makes six ½-cup servings.

OATMEAL CRISP

1½ cups all-purpose flour
¾ cup light brown sugar
1½ cups old-fashioned oats
1 teaspoon fine sea salt
½ teaspoon ground cinnamon
⅛ teaspoon ground nutmeg
2 sticks (8 ounces) unsalted
        butter, chilled and cut
        into small pieces

Preheat oven to 350°F. In a large bowl, blend the flour, brown sugar, oats, salt, cinnamon and nutmeg. Using your fingers, "pinch" the butter into the ingredients. The mixture should be crumbly. Spread evenly on a lined baking sheet. Bake for 20 minutes, or until lightly browned. For even browning, stir the oats or rotate the pan midway through cooking. With a spatula, carefully toss the mixture to create chunks of crisp. Let cool uncovered. This can be stored in an airtight container in your pantry for up to 2 weeks.

Earl Grey

⅓ cup loose whole-leaf Earl Grey tea
2 cups whole milk
¾ cup granulated sugar
¼ teaspoon fine sea salt
2 tablespoons golden syrup (page 13)
1½ cups heavy whipping cream

In a medium saucepan, combine the tea leaves and milk. Bring to a simmer over medium-high heat (small bubbles will form), stirring occasionally. Remove from the heat and let steep for 15 minutes. Strain into a bowl using a fine sieve. Add the sugar, salt, golden syrup and cream. Stir with a spoon until the sugar dissolves, using a quick circular motion without creating foam. This will take a few minutes. Pour into a container, cover, and refrigerate until chilled.

For each serving, stir and then pour ½ cup of the chilled mixture into the Sweet Spot. Stir until frozen and serve.

Makes six ½-cup servings.

Top with a drizzle of lemon curd and serve with shortbread cookies.

Brown Butter Pecan

1½ cups whole milk
1½ cups heavy whipping cream
½ cup granulated sugar
¼ cup light brown sugar
¼ teaspoon fine sea salt
2 tablespoons golden syrup (page 13)
1 teaspoon pure vanilla extract
¼ teaspoon almond extract
6 to 12 tablespoons coarsely chopped roasted pecans
(page 80)

In a bowl, combine all ingredients except the pecans.
Stir with a spoon until the sugars dissolve, using
a quick circular motion without creating foam. This
will take a few minutes. Pour into a container, cover,
and refrigerate until chilled.

If adding the optional Brown Butter Bits, stir them into
the chilled mixture. For each serving, stir and then pour
½ cup of the chilled mixture into the Sweet Spot. Once
it is ¾ frozen, fold in 1 to 2 tablespoons pecans.

Makes six ½-cup servings.

BROWN BUTTER BITS

½ cup unsalted butter

In a heavy-bottomed
saucepan, melt the butter
over medium heat,
stirring to brown evenly.
As the butter heats up,
it will begin to foam. The
color will change from
pale yellow to nut-brown.
As the nut-brown color
begins to show, take the
pan off the heat. The
butter will continue to
brown. Let it stand for
a few minutes until the
browning stops. The
butter will be separated.
Skim off the clear
(clarified) butter for use
in other cooking. Use the
browned butter solids at
the bottom of the pan for
the ice cream mixture.

It's autumn now and acorns scatter over soft ground.

Socked feet dance and bellies laugh in the kitchen.

Almond Fudge Ribbon

1½ cups whole milk
1½ cups heavy whipping cream
½ cup granulated sugar
⅛ teaspoon fine sea salt
2 tablespoons golden syrup (page 13)
⅛ teaspoon natural almond extract
6 tablespoons Chocolate Fudge Topping (page 82)

In a mixing bowl, combine all ingredients except the topping. Stir with a spoon until the sugar dissolves, using a quick circular motion without creating foam. This will take a few minutes. Pour into a container, cover, and refrigerate until chilled.

For each serving, stir and then pour ½ cup of the chilled mixture into the Sweet Spot. Once it is ¾ frozen, fold in 1 tablespoon Chocolate Fudge Topping and 1 tablespoon coarsely chopped roasted almonds.

Makes six ½-cup servings.

ROASTED ALMONDS

¾ cup raw almonds
1 tablespoon unsalted butter, melted
½ teaspoon fine sea salt

Preheat oven to 350°F. In a mixing bowl, toss the nuts, butter and salt until well coated. Spread evenly on a lined sheet pan. Place the pan on the middle oven rack. Bake until lightly browned and fragrant, about 10 minutes. Let cool to room temperature. These can be stored in a sealed container for up to 2 weeks. Coarsely chop with a knife before using.

Avocado Horchata

1 cup avocado pulp (from 1 large avocado, soft to the touch)
1 cup coconut milk
1 teaspoon ground cinnamon
Juice of 1 lime
1 cup almond milk
½ cup granulated sugar
2 tablespoons golden syrup (page 13)
½ teaspoon fine sea salt
½ teaspoon pure vanilla extract

In a blender, combine the avocado, coconut milk, cinnamon and lime juice. Blend until pureed. Pour the avocado mixture into a bowl. Add the almond milk, sugar, golden syrup, salt and vanilla. Stir with a spoon until the sugar dissolves, using a quick circular motion without creating foam. This will take a few minutes. Pour into a container, cover, and refrigerate until chilled.

For each serving, stir and then pour ½ cup of the chilled mixture into the Sweet Spot. Stir until frozen and serve.

Makes six ½-cup servings.

Top with a spoonful of Caramel Topping. Page 82

Dream of green gold south of the Rio Grande.

Honey Lemon Sorbet

2 tablespoons grated lemon zest (about 2 to 4 lemons)
2 cups fresh lemon juice (5 to 7 lemons)
½ cup water, room temperature or chilled
½ teaspoon pure vanilla extract
½ cup honey
¾ cup granulated sugar

In a mixing bowl, combine all ingredients and stir until the sugar dissolves. This will take a few minutes. Pour into a container, cover, and refrigerate until chilled.

For each serving, stir and then pour ½ cup of the chilled mixture into the Sweet Spot. Stir until frozen and serve.

Makes six ½-cup servings.

Gently fold in fresh raspberries while freezing for a flavor twist.

Like a morning bird on a blue sky day, a burst of lemon sings.

Pineapple Spice Sorbet

½ fresh pineapple, peeled and cored
1 cup pineapple juice
½ teaspoon ground black pepper
⅛ teaspoon ground turmeric
⅛ teaspoon ground cardamom
¾ cup granulated sugar
⅓ cup golden syrup (page 13)
3 tablespoons lime juice (about 1 to 2 limes)
1½ teaspoons peeled and grated fresh ginger
1 teaspoon coarsely chopped fresh mint leaves

In a blender, puree the pineapple with the pineapple juice. In a small bowl, mix the black pepper, turmeric and cardamom with the sugar.

In a mixing bowl, combine the pineapple puree, spiced sugar mix, golden syrup, lime juice, grated ginger and mint. Stir with a spoon until the sugar dissolves and the spices are evenly distributed, using a quick circular motion without creating foam. This will take a few minutes. Pour into a container, cover, and refrigerate until chilled.

For each serving, stir and then pour ½ cup of the chilled mixture into the Sweet Spot. Stir until frozen and serve.

Makes six ½-cup servings.

Take a deep breath of summer:
the yellow sun, the turquoise water, and the white sand.

Coffee

1¼ cups whole milk, divided
2 teaspoons instant coffee
¾ cup granulated sugar
¼ teaspoon fine sea salt
2 tablespoons golden syrup (page 13)
1¾ cups heavy whipping cream
2 teaspoons pure vanilla extract
2 tablespoons finely ground French roast coffee beans (optional)

In a small saucepan, warm ¼ cup milk over medium heat for 1 to 2 minutes, or until warm to the touch (about 110°F). Stir in the instant coffee until dissolved.

In a large mixing bowl, combine the remaining milk, sugar, salt, golden syrup, cream, vanilla and the warm coffee mixture. Stir with a spoon until the sugar dissolves, using a quick circular motion without creating foam. This will take a few minutes. Pour into a container, cover, and refrigerate until chilled.

For each serving, stir and then pour ½ cup of the chilled mixture into the Sweet Spot. For an added "bean" experience, while freezing fold in 1 teaspoon finely ground coffee beans.

Makes six ½-cup servings.

For a richer coffee flavor, add 1 more teaspoon instant coffee to the base.

Take in the taste of Seattle, straight out of Pike Place Market.

1 cup granulated sugar
2 tablespoons golden syrup (page 13)
¼ cup water
4 tablespoons salted butter, sliced into 4 pieces
1¾ cups whole milk
1¼ cups heavy whipping cream
2 teaspoons malted milk powder
2 teaspoons finely ground dark-roast coffee beans (espresso grind)
¼ teaspoon ground coriander
¼ teaspoon ground cinnamon

Pastry brush and cup of warm water

Prepare a buttered, lined sheet pan. Set aside.

In a heavy-bottomed saucepan, combine the sugar, golden syrup and water. Stir until well blended. Dip the pastry brush in the warm water and brush down the sides of the pan to remove any sugar crystals. This is an important step to prevent sugar crystals from forming. Bring to a rolling boil over medium-high heat and cook until the temperature is 300° to 310°F, about 6 to 10 minutes. It will become copper-colored and aromatic. Remove from the heat immediately. Stir in 2 pieces of the butter until melted. Return to the stove over medium heat. Add the remaining butter one piece at a time, stirring until each is fully incorporated. Remove from the heat. Pour half of the mixture onto the prepared sheet pan. Set aside to cool.

Immediately return the saucepan to the stove with the remaining half of the still-warm toffee. Over medium heat, slowly and carefully stir the milk into the warm toffee until all the toffee is dissolved. Watch out for steam. Remove from the heat. Stir in the cream, malted milk powder, coffee, coriander and cinnamon. Pour into a container, cover, and refrigerate until chilled.

When the toffee on the sheet pan has cooled, break into smaller pieces and place in a food processor. Pulse into fine pieces. This can be stored in an airtight container for several weeks.

For each serving, stir and then pour ½ cup of the chilled mixture into the Sweet Spot. Once it is ¾ frozen, fold in 2 teaspoons of toffee bits.

Makes six ½-cup servings.

Serve on top of a freshly baked brownie for a dessert you'll remember.

While rain taps the window pane, cozy up with a good book and your favorite coffee brewing.

Macadamia Mango Sherbet

1 cup mango puree (about 2 ripe mangoes, aromatic and soft to the touch, or
thawed frozen mango)
1½ cups whole milk
¼ cup heavy whipping cream
¾ cup mango smoothie, any brand
⅓ cup light brown sugar
¼ teaspoon fine sea salt
2 tablespoons golden syrup (page 13)
¼ cup orange juice concentrate
2 tablespoons fresh lemon juice (about 1 small lemon)
12 tablespoons chopped roasted macadamia nuts (page 80)

Place the mango in a blender with the milk. Blend until smooth. Transfer the mixture to a large mixing bowl and add the remaining ingredients except the nuts. Stir with a spoon until the sugar dissolves, using a quick circular motion without creating foam. This will take a few minutes. Note: If any small unbreakable sugar lumps remain, remove them. Pour the mixture into a container, cover, and refrigerate until chilled.

For each serving, stir and then pour ½ cup of the chilled mixture into the Sweet Spot. Once it is ¾ frozen, fold in 2 tablespoons roasted macadamia nuts.

Makes six ½-cup servings.

You don't need to know the hula to have a luau.

Rocky Toffee Road

3 ounces dark chocolate, broken into small pieces (or ¾ cup semisweet or
        bittersweet chocolate chips)
¼ cup plus ⅓ cup granulated sugar
¼ cup Dutch-process cocoa powder
1⅓ cups whole milk
1⅔ cups heavy whipping cream
¼ teaspoon fine sea salt
2 tablespoons golden syrup (page 13)
1 teaspoon pure vanilla extract
12 tablespoons coarsely chopped Almond Butter Toffee (page 81)
6 to 12 tablespoons marshmallow creme

Place the chocolate pieces in a large heatproof mixing bowl. Set aside. In a small
bowl, blend ¼ cup sugar and the cocoa. Set aside.

In a heavy-bottomed saucepan, combine the milk, whipping cream, ⅓ cup sugar, salt
and golden syrup. Stir with a spoon until the sugar begins to dissolve, using a quick
circular motion without creating foam. This will take a few minutes. Cook over
medium heat for 6 to 8 minutes, or until steam rises and small bubbles begin to form
around the edges. Remove from the heat *prior* to boiling. Carefully pour the heated
milk mixture over the chocolate pieces. Let stand for 3 to 5 minutes to fully melt the
chocolate. Whisk until smooth. Blend in the cocoa mixture. When fully incorporated,
stir in the vanilla. Pour into a container, cover, and refrigerate until chilled.

For each serving, stir and then pour ½ cup of the chilled mixture into the Sweet
Spot. Once it is ¾ frozen, fold in 2 tablespoons Almond Butter Toffee and 1 to 2
tablespoons marshmallow creme.

Makes six ½-cup servings.

If the moon is made of cheese,
then mountains are made of marshmallows.

Chocolate Banana Malt

1¼ cups whole milk
1¾ cups heavy whipping cream
¼ teaspoon fine sea salt
2 tablespoons golden syrup (page 13)
¾ cup chocolate syrup
¼ cup malted milk powder
1 ripe banana, pureed

In a mixing bowl, combine the milk, cream, salt and golden syrup. Stir with a spoon until the syrup is completely blended, using a quick circular motion without creating foam. This will take a few minutes. Stir in the chocolate syrup. Add the malted milk powder and banana puree, stirring until fully incorporated. Pour into a container, cover, and refrigerate until chilled.

For each serving, stir and then pour ½ cup of the chilled mixture into the Sweet Spot. Stir until frozen and serve.

Makes six ½-cup servings.

Replace the malted milk powder with 1 to 2 tablespoons coarsely crushed malted milk ball candies for each serving. Add when the mixture is nearly frozen.

Smiles can't help but skate across children's faces.

Caramel Apple

1 cup whole milk
1 cup heavy whipping cream
½ cup granulated sugar
¼ teaspoon fine sea salt
2 tablespoons golden syrup (page 13)
6 tablespoons Caramel Topping (page 82)

In a bowl, combine all
ingredients except the topping.
Stir with a spoon until the sugar
dissolves, using a quick circular motion
without creating foam. This will take
a few minutes. Stir in the Caramelized
Apples. Pour into a container, cover, and refrigerate until chilled.

For each serving, stir and then pour ½ cup of the chilled mixture
into the Sweet Spot. Once it is ¾ frozen, fold in 1 tablespoon Caramel
Topping.

Makes six ½-cup servings.

CARAMELIZED APPLES

1 cup peeled, cored and coarsely chopped tart apples (2 medium Granny Smiths)
¼ cup light brown sugar
1 tablespoon unsalted butter, melted
1 teaspoon ground cinnamon

Preheat oven to 400°F. In a bowl, combine all ingredients and toss until well coated.
Spread the apple mixture in a single layer on a lined baking sheet. Bake for 15
minutes, or until the apples are golden brown and coated with melted sugar. Let cool.

If October were any dessert,
it would be a caramel apple.

Generations gather at hom

Pumpkin Pie

⅔ cup dark brown sugar
1 teaspoon ground cinnamon
½ teaspoon ground cloves
½ teaspoon ground ginger
1 teaspoon fine sea salt
1 cup pumpkin puree, canned or fresh roasted
1¼ cups whole milk
1¼ cups heavy whipping cream
2 tablespoons golden syrup (page 13)
1 teaspoon pure vanilla extract

To "dress up" for the holidays, garnish with crushed butter toffee. Substitute pecans for the almonds in the recipe, page 81. Drizzle with Caramel Topping, page 82, to top it off.

In a large bowl, combine the brown sugar, cinnamon, cloves, ginger and salt. Stir in the pumpkin puree. Add the remaining ingredients, stirring with a spoon until the sugar dissolves. Pour into a container, cover, and refrigerate until chilled.

For each serving, stir and then pour ½ cup of the chilled mixture into the Sweet Spot. Stir until frozen and serve.

Makes six ½-cup servings.

ROASTED PUMPKIN

For rich depth of flavor, use fresh roasted pumpkin: Preheat oven to 375°F. Cut a sugar pie pumpkin or butternut squash from tip to toe and remove the seeds. Place the two halves cut-side down on a buttered sheet pan. Bake for 40 to 50 minutes, or until fork-tender. Let cool. Scoop out the roasted meat and puree. Refrigerate.

The children giggle while the old folks start to doze.

Peppermint Crunch

1½ cups whole milk
1½ cups heavy whipping cream
¾ cup granulated sugar
¼ teaspoon fine sea salt
2 tablespoons golden syrup (page 13)
3 to 4 drops pure peppermint oil (see note)
¾ cup coarsely chopped peppermint hard candy

In a mixing bowl, combine the milk, cream, sugar, salt, golden syrup and peppermint oil. Stir with a spoon until the sugar dissolves, using a quick circular motion without creating foam. This will take a few minutes. Pour into a container, cover, and refrigerate until chilled.

For each serving, stir and then pour ½ cup of the chilled mixture into the Sweet Spot. Sprinkle with 2 tablespoons chopped peppermint candy while freezing. Stir until frozen and serve.

Makes six ½-cup servings.

Note: Peppermint oil has a much more concentrated flavor than peppermint extract. You can substitute 2 teaspoons of peppermint extract for the peppermint oil in this recipe.

If you don't have a food processor to chop the hard candies, place them inside a clean, folded towel and crush with a rolling pin.

Now the wrapping paper is strewn across the floor like confetti.

Your ice cream deserves the royal treatment.

FINISHING TOUCHES

* Roasted Nuts
* Almond Butter Toffee
* Chocolate Fudge Topping
* Caramel Topping

Roasted Nuts

1 cup raw nuts, unsalted and shelled
1 tablespoon unsalted butter, melted
½ teaspoon fine sea salt

Preheat oven to 350°F. In a mixing bowl, combine the
nuts, butter and salt. Toss until well coated. Spread
evenly on a lined sheet pan. Place the pan on the
middle oven rack. Bake until lightly browned and
fragrant, about 10 minutes. Let cool to room
temperature, then coarsely chop.

Pecans,
pistachios and
macadamia nuts are
simple to roast. Store
in a sealed container
for up to 2
weeks.

Cozy feelings stir when we breathe that savory aroma.

Almond Butter Toffee

1 cup sliced almonds, roasted and coarsely chopped, divided
½ cup granulated sugar
½ cup light brown sugar
½ cup golden syrup (page 13)
¼ cup water
½ cup unsalted butter, sliced into 8 pieces
1 teaspoon pure vanilla extract

Any nuts
or seeds can
be used in this
recipe.

Pastry brush and cup of warm water

Place a buttered nonstick liner on a sheet pan.
Spread ½ cup of the roasted almonds on the lined sheet pan. Set aside.

In a heavy-bottomed saucepan, combine the sugar, brown sugar, golden syrup and water. Stir until well blended. Dip the pastry brush in the warm water and brush down the sides of the pan to remove any sugar crystals. This is an important step to prevent sugar crystals from forming. Bring to a rolling boil over medium-high heat and cook until the temperature is 300° to 305°F, about 6 to 10 minutes. It will become copper-colored and aromatic. Remove from the heat. Add 2 pieces of the butter one slice at a time, stirring until each piece is incorporated. Return the mixture to the stove over medium heat. Add the remaining butter one slice at a time, stirring until incorporated. Remove from the heat. Stir in the vanilla.

Quickly pour the hot mixture over the ½ cup roasted almonds on the sheet pan. Evenly spread the toffee with a buttered offset spatula. Sprinkle the remaining ½ cup roasted almonds over the toffee. With the spatula, firmly press them into the toffee. Let cool, then break the toffee into small pieces. Store in an airtight container for several days.

Chocolate Fudge Topping

1 cup semisweet chocolate chips (51% cacao or more)
½ cup whole evaporated milk
¼ cup heavy whipping cream
1 teaspoon pure vanilla extract

Place the chocolate chips in a heatproof bowl. Set aside. In a medium saucepan, combine the evaporated milk and cream. Cook over medium heat for 2 to 3 minutes, or until steam rises and small bubbles begin to form around the edges. Remove from the heat *prior* to boiling. Carefully pour the heated milk over the chocolate chips. Let stand without stirring for 3 minutes to soften the chocolate. Whisk briskly until the sauce is smooth. Mix in the vanilla. Pour into a container, cover, and refrigerate overnight, or until the chocolate is set. It will thicken into a spoonable fudge topping. Store in the refrigerator for up to 2 weeks.

Caramel Topping

1 cup granulated sugar
2 tablespoons golden syrup
     (page 13)
¼ cup water
2 tablespoons unsalted butter
¾ cup heavy whipping cream
½ teaspoon fine sea salt
1 teaspoon pure vanilla extract

Pastry brush
Cup of warm water

In a heavy-bottomed saucepan, combine the sugar, golden syrup and water. Stir until well blended. Dip the pastry brush in the warm water and brush down the sides of the pan to remove any sugar crystals. This is an important step to prevent sugar crystals from forming. Bring to a rolling boil over medium-high heat and cook until the temperature is 305° to 310°F, about 6 to 10 minutes. It will become copper-colored and aromatic. Remove from the heat. Add the butter, stirring until incorporated. Slowly and carefully stir in the cream. Watch out for steam. Stir in the salt and vanilla. Pour into a container, cover, and refrigerate until chilled. It will thicken into a spoonable topping. Stored in the refrigerator for up to a month.

*The sound of joy
is the clink of spoons on bowls.*

For a pourable
chocolate or caramel
sauce, stir 2 teaspoons
of milk into ½ cup
of topping.

ICED DRINKS

* Iced Mimosa
* Bloody Mary Granita
* Lemon Drop Ice
* Ginger Beer Sorbet
* Margarita

Good friends and great laughs are all you need for

celebration.

Iced Mimosa

2 tablespoons lemon juice (about 1 small lemon)
2½ cups fresh orange juice
¼ cup granulated sugar
⅓ cup orange marmalade
2 tablespoons golden syrup (page 13)
1½ cups sparkling wine, chilled

6 champagne flutes, chilled

In a mixing bowl, combine the lemon juice, orange juice, sugar, marmalade and golden syrup. Whisk until blended and the sugar dissolves. Pour into a container, cover, and refrigerate until chilled.

For each serving, stir the chilled mixture well to disperse the orange peel and then pour ½ cup into the Sweet Spot. When it is frozen, place the mimosa in a chilled champagne flute. Pour ¼ cup of sparkling wine over the ice.

Makes six ½-cup servings.

Maple syrup scents the air, and French toast gra

rm plates. Cheers!

There's no such thing as too early, is there?

Bloody Mary Granita

2½ cups tomato-vegetable juice blend
2 tablespoons tomato paste
2 tablespoons golden syrup
2 tablespoons lemon juice (about 1 small lemon)
2 tablespoons Worcestershire sauce
2 tablespoons green olive brine
2 teaspoons Dijon mustard
1 teaspoon minced garlic
1 teaspoon Old Bay seasoning
1 teaspoon hot sauce
½ teaspoon smoked paprika
½ teaspoon freshly ground black pepper
6 ounces premium vodka, chilled

6 glasses, chilled

Garnish options:
Julienned celery ribs with leaves
Pickled green beans or asparagus
Green olives and pickled onions on a skewer
Jumbo prawns, cooked
Diced tomato

A teaspoon of finely grated horseradish adds a nice twist that can be either added to or substituted for the mustard.

In a large bowl, combine all ingredients except the vodka. Whisk until fully blended. Pour into a container, cover, and refrigerate until chilled.

For each serving, stir and then pour ½ cup of the chilled mixture into the Sweet Spot. When it is frozen, add 1 ounce chilled vodka to a chilled glass. With a rounded scoop, add the granita to the glass. Garnish as desired.

Makes six ½-cup servings.

Lemon Drop Ice

2 tablespoons grated lemon zest (about 2 to 4 lemons)
2 cups fresh lemon juice (about 8 large or 16 small lemons)
½ cup water
½ cup granulated sugar
⅔ cup golden syrup (page 13)
½ teaspoon pure vanilla extract
6 ounces premium vodka, chilled

6 cocktail glasses, chilled

In a mixing bowl, combine the lemon zest and juice, water, sugar, golden syrup and vanilla. Whisk until the sugar dissolves. This will take a few minutes. Pour into a container, cover, and refrigerate until chilled.

For each serving, stir and then pour ½ cup of the chilled mixture into the Sweet Spot. Stir until frozen.

To serve, pour 1 ounce chilled vodka into each chilled cocktail glass. Add a ½-cup serving of Lemon Drop Ice.

Makes six ½-cup servings.

For sweet-tart sipping, moisten the rim of your chilled cocktail glass with a cut lemon, then dip the rim in a saucer of sugar before adding the vodka and Lemon Drop Ice.

Under a disco globe, shimmering hips dip and pink petal lips pucker up.

Ginger Beer Sorbet

3 tablespoons peeled and finely grated fresh ginger
½ cup lemon juice (about 2 large lemons)
⅓ cup granulated sugar
2 tablespoons golden syrup (page 13)
2 cups ginger beer (or ginger ale)

In a mixing bowl, combine the ginger, lemon juice, sugar, golden syrup and ginger beer. Whisk until the sugar dissolves. This will take a few minutes. Pour into a container, cover, and refrigerate until chilled.

For each serving, stir and then pour ½ cup of the chilled mixture into the Sweet Spot. Stir until frozen and serve.

Makes six ½-cup servings.

Before juicing, soften the lemons by hand-rolling on a hard surface.

A cool fizz refreshes on a lazy July weekend.

Margarita

2 tablespoons grated lime zest (about 4 to 6 limes)
1½ cups fresh lime juice (about 9 limes)
½ cup fresh orange juice
⅓ cup water
½ cup golden syrup (page 13)
⅓ cup granulated sugar
6 ounces silver tequila, chilled
3 ounces orange liqueur, chilled

6 cocktail glasses, chilled, rimmed with fine sea salt if desired

In a bowl, combine the lime zest and juice, orange juice, water, golden syrup and sugar. Whisk until the sugar dissolves. This will take a few minutes. Pour into a container, cover, and refrigerate until chilled.

For a little saltiness, moisten the rim of your chilled glass with a cut lime, then dip the rim in a saucer of salt before adding the Margarita.

For each serving, stir and then pour ½ cup of the chilled mixture into the Sweet Spot. Stir until frozen.

To serve, pour 2 tablespoons tequila and 1 tablespoon orange liqueur into each chilled cocktail glass. Add a ½-cup serving of Margarita ice.

Makes six ½-cup servings.

Tú tienes mi corazón.

There's no end to creativity